iona of my heart
iona of my love

instead of monk's voices
will be lowing of cattle

but 'ere the world ends
iona shall be as it was

~ st. columba

portraits

OF

iona

AN ARTIST'S PERSPECTIVE
IN PAINT AND PROSE

by kari gale

FOR CYNDI AND FOR ALEX
MY HEART IS GLAD YOU FOUND REST ON IONA

In January of 2016 in the midst of what would turn out to be fifteen months of travel, I flew to the UK with only a vague idea of exactly where I was headed. I initially considered immersing myself in the art and culture of a big city, perhaps in the beauty of Edinburgh or the bustle of Glasgow. I wanted to feel the energy and vitality I associated with a thriving metropolis and the dynamic diversity of the people who live there.

To my surprise, I ended up living in a tiny shepherd's bothy overlooking the sea on an island off the coast of Scotland. This city girl subsequently came to love Iona, a remote island in the inner Hebrides. I came to participate in an art residency for the month of February; I left realizing I had unearthed a part of myself that had been hidden and secreted away. I learned I could feel at home in a small community and find great pleasure in simple daily routines. I found a strange new world of contentment. Less became more and with the less came peace. I began to imagine how I could carry this surprising new feeling with me back to the states. I examined my life in a new way, with new eyes.

I am a journal artist. My journal illustrations are my memories, my experiences, life captured in slow motion. I learned to love this particular form of art in 2013 when I walked five hundred miles on the Camino de Santiago across Northern Spain. In the process, I found myself not just documenting my travels, but capturing the essence of the journey. Three years after completing the Camino, I had filled up a myriad of journals with sketches and even published a book of illustrations from that first pilgrimage to Santiago de Compostela.

The weather in Iona in winter couldn't have been more different from the warmth of Spain in summer. I had never tried to draw outside in such frigid temperatures. On Iona I learned to sketch quickly, with minimal line work.

The residency required me to host a small art show, so I decided to use a larger pad of watercolour paper to create paintings I could display in addition to my journal art. When I left the island, I had completed about twenty drawings. I wrote the following in my journal on March 9th:

"I left Iona today. Blazing sunlight warmed my back through my fleece as I climbed to the highest point on the island, Dun I, to say goodbye. You can see the entire island from this viewpoint and far across the water to Skye on a clear day. I'm not sad to leave, because I have a strong feeling I'm going to return in the fall. When I had my open studio last Friday, the local folks that attended were so encouraging and thought that Iona should be the subject for my next book. I don't know exactly what will happen in the next few months, but it is a strong and lovely possibility. Iona feels a lot like 'home.' I love the idea of coming back and creating more art that could fill a book. The idea of pilgrimage continues to fascinate me and Iona has been a place that pilgrims have sought even longer than Santiago de Compostela. Where the Camino is a pilgrimage of movement, Iona seems to be a pilgrimage of waiting and listening. I'm getting good at forward movement. I could use some practice on the rest."

I did return. I came back for six more weeks in November before finally flying home to the states at the end of 2016. The body of work I had started in February felt unfinished and my fingers itched to capture more of the landscape, more of the character, more portraits of Iona. This book is the result of those combined ten weeks. The words and the stories that accompany these images are gathered from many sources, including long and leisurely conversations, the pages of my journal, and the moments when I sat alone on the edge of the sea and tried to let the essence of Iona seep into me.

the nunnery

is the first ruin encountered on Iona.
The wall in my painting is set sharply
against the blue of the sky, with crumbling
rock creating a contrast to the stark
angles jutting heavenward.

I like these ruins a lot, perhaps even better than the Abbey, which is the more
famous. I sit on the remains of the walls in the afternoon sunshine,
imagining the nuns going about their lives some seven hundred years ago.

The outside surface of this building looks smooth and flat, but from where I sit
drawing I can see the vast amounts of rock that have been used to construct each
wall. It's hard to believe that when so many varied stones are placed just so, they can
be used to build an entire structure.

Drawings and words are my own stones. I use each one, and stack them just so, to
create a unique picture of Iona—this artist's perspective of a place that is sacred for
many reasons: its history, land, sea and sky. I want to share with you what captured
my eye and my heart, and why I documented these scenes on paper. I want to share
with you the magic of Iona through ink and paint, as well as some simple stories. If
you haven't visited Iona, perhaps you will be inspired to see the island with your own
eyes. If you have, my hope is that you will be able to see the island anew, and carry a
piece of it with you.

overlooking
the beach from
Hugh's bench.

If I never walked farther than the sands of Traigh na Criche, the trip to Iona would still have been worthwhile. Being used to the grey beaches of Oregon, on the northwest coast of the United States, it is strange to see the many distant islands of the Inner Hebrides gleaming in the unexpected February sunshine.

On my first morning on Iona, I discover a bench that gives me a full view of this pristine stretch of sand and rock, and I sit down to draw. There are many such benches scattered around the island. They all invite reflection; a quiet meditation of heaven and earth. Many are dedicated to loved ones, and I have chosen Hugh's bench. As the wind pinks my cheeks, I quickly sketch the important lines, eager to add colours that seem almost too bright for a winter scene.

perched on cnoc mor

a few day later, overlooking the southern half of Iona,
I choose vivid chartreuse greens and deep indigo blues
to capture the luminous tapestry spread below me.

Many will tell you that
the light on Iona is extraordinary;
perhaps unearthly.

I must say…
I completely agree.

The view from
the top of Cnoc
Mor looking South

Painting the entrance to the
Iona Abbey. Crisp bitter wind whips
round my ears! Hands frozen but
Pen moving swiftly.

Time stands still
in reverence of
this sacred holy
    Presence
in the midst of
this crystalline
winter day.
Azure &
Turquoise.
Grass green.
Stone.
beauty.

the iona abbey

is the subject of my first drawing
on my new larger pad of watercolour paper.

It is a modest stone building surrounded by Celtic crosses and gentle grass hills.
The coastline of the Isle of Mull is set behind it, with a ribbon of deep turquoise
and cobalt separating the two islands.

In other famous churches one is dwarfed by lofty ceilings, sweeping arches, and
a vast magnificence that overwhelms the senses. These churches were designed to
make one feel small in the midst of God's grandeur. In contrast, the Iona Abbey
invites reflection, prayer and stillness. The centuries of history lived out in these
walls give the Abbey a profound presence, yet it is still approachable and welcoming.

I believe that God is always near and is waiting for us to see Him.
I believe this is true all of the time, but on Iona it feels more tangible.
More palpable.

I see the Divine everywhere; in the marks on the stones, the wool of the sheep, and
the patterns the waves leave in the sand. On Iona, God may meet you in front of the
Abbey altar, but then He walks with you out into the blustery February afternoon to
peer into tidal pools and watch birds dance on the wind.

On the same day I draw the entrance, I explore the inside of the Abbey and sit down in a small alcove known as 'the Quiet Corner.' On the window sill is an open notebook labeled the 'Iona Abbey Worship Book.' It contains a selection of quotes and scriptures listed for each day of the month. One of the scriptures for this particular day is Psalm 46:10.

Be still and know that I am God.

I think this will be my verse for the time I am on Iona.
My meditation. I want to rest in this verse.
I want it to quiet my fears and fill up my heart.

Be still and know that I am God.

be still

I will start with that.

sheep finally staying
still allowing me to capture
them on paper. They appear bemused.

The View from
the bothy window
watching it all afternoon
while I luxuriate
in a novel:
every few minutes
it changes
and changes
and changes
again.

the wind blows

rattling the joints of the bothy
I am snug and warm in my wee cave

rain pelting against the window
the bothy occasionally sways in resistance to the bullying of the gales
but we are anchored and steady here in our little bog overlooking the sea

listening to the Wailin' Jennys
feels just right...
harmony, melancholy
but sweet and warm

The last three days have been glorious. Beautiful blue skies with bright sunshine that will warm your skin if you find a sheltered spot away from the wind. I am sinking into peace more and more each day.

I've been staying in the bothy

It is equipped with a comfy twin bed, cupboard and shelves for storage, and a bedside table and lamp. It also has a small chair and table for me to work at, an electric kettle, and most importantly, a heater. It is a powerful little space heater that keeps me toasty when winter storms pound the island with rain and sleet during the night.

I use the hostel for showering and cooking as it is just a short stroll down the hill. It has been lovely to have my own private retreat for painting and writing, and I am enchanted with my cozy space. John, the owner of the bothy and the hostel, has decorated it with thick plaid blankets, curtains and beautiful art, and I am so grateful to call it home for the time I am here.

Speaking of time, it is going too fast. I've spent two weeks on Iona as of tomorrow. The days themselves, however, feel leisurely and wonderfully slow. I spend my days painting and walking and exploring the island. I get up when I wake up, and I go to bed when I am tired. This alone is quite magical. I make tea and porridge and then head out for the day. I carry my journal with me in my backpack as well as my larger pad of watercolour paper. I usually start several drawings during the day and try to finish the ink lines and add colour to the sketches when I return to the bothy later in the evening. I have always been a bit of a night owl so sometimes I curl up under the blankets and paint in bed before I turn out the light.

I stagger along pushing against the wall of wind that whips sand in my face and chills my ears. The grass flails wildly and is instantly pressed down, subdued by the weight of the gale. Placid sheep graze in the valley between the dunes. I share their respite from the elements until they startle and quickly disappear over the next rise.

the sea is untamed

Vast waves crash against volcanic rock creating white sprays of foam that become a storm of cotton floating towards me, catching in bogs and between cragged rocks. I turn my back on the wind and she pushes me. She won't be ignored. I feel pressed and hurried as my feet step and shuffle to catch up. I look back to see the watercolour edge of the grey-blue cloud drift closer. I secure my hood a bit tighter and follow the faint path home.

I first see neil's boat

in the middle of February, It sits on blocks near the pier, receiving a fresh coat of paint. The harbour on Iona is small, colourful, and full of life even in the middle of winter. The ferries are the star of the show, moving back and forth on their appointed route across the narrow stretch of water between Iona and Fionnaphort.

In November, Neil's boat is out in the harbour sporting her new colours. After drawing something, I feel like I have a special connection to it. Somehow, this fishing boat is like an old friend I asked to pose for me—one with a wonderful penchant for sitting very, very still.

I love walking
past this view.
Every day the blue
changes. Today it
was azure, deep
and heavy in contrast
to the sparkling gems
of muel, looking rose
gold across the water.
That little house must have
the most magnificent of
all views. It wakes
every morning to the
kaleidoscope of light &
colors as the clouds
and mist dance across
the sky. Lucky house.

Iona Wool
the heart of the
island

During the first six months of
my travels I painted two to three
times a week, but on Iona I *paint every day*

Perching on high hilltops, sandy beaches and precarious rocks, I put pen to paper to
draw what is before me. I feel a bit out of my comfort zone when attempting larger
pieces, but have noticed that throughout the process I am honing my technique and
getting more adept at choosing subject matter that works best with my artistic style.
Working in a journal helps me not take myself so seriously, but with a large piece of
crisp white official watercolour paper poised on my lap, I get a bit overwhelmed; as
if this paper converts the bearer to an italicised '*artist*' instead of just someone who
likes to sketch.

I am learning to accept that one doesn't have to be good at drawing everything. I'm
also learning to give myself permission to identify early on the subjects that will
bring me joy to draw and not worry about the rest. Learning one's limitations can
ultimately be so freeing.

I love capturing the textures and colours of Iona: the jagged shapes of rocks lining the beaches, saturated in deep red, burnt orange, soft grey, and mossy green; the warm ochre and muted celadon of the undulating machair; the rich muddy brown punctuating the swell and rise of the bogs, ground seeping and wet with winter rain.

and then there is the sea
oh, the sea

Intense turquoise and cobalt transform in minutes to a pale ice blue that morphs into indigo towards the horizon. All of this beauty is ever changing under clouds that sweep and billow over Iona. They scowl, moody and dark with rain and sleet one moment, then suddenly split open to reveal a vivid sun that lights up the entire landscape from within, glowing and sparkling, breathing and pulsing.

the
blue
room

When I first contacted John, I was emailing him about becoming an artist in residence. All I really knew about John was that he ran the hostel. It turns out he also has a herd of black sheep.

I arrive on the last ferry from Mull and John picks me up in his car, driving through the blackness to the north end of the island. As he deposits me at the door of the hostel, he invites me and the volunteers who work there up to his house for a movie night. I gladly agree, eager to meet the people who will become my community for the following four weeks.

When I enter John's house, and specifically his living room, I am stunned. This room, which I henceforth call 'the blue room,' is captivating. I feel like I have just entered a tiny, well curated museum. The walls are painted a bold sapphire with accents of jade green and shimmering gold. Each piece exhibited—from the couch and the coffee table, to the extensive paintings and art—are carefully positioned and lit. The artistry in the presentation and selection is masterful, yet the room still feels cozy and comfortable.

I sink down into the pillows on the sofa eagerly taking in each colour and shape. I feel honoured to be invited to enter into this space. John pours some wine and puts in the movie and we all settle in. As the light dims, I know that I want to paint this space. I want to capture this creative expression of who John is.

It's not that often you find a shepherd who runs a hostel and is also a talented interior designer. But I am less surprised by these things now. Slow travel does that to you; it opens you up. You learn to set judgement aside and allow a person to share who they are, piece by piece, in their own time. Sometimes, you are lucky enough to get invited into a blue room.

Trying something new with an animal portrait. I am enrap-tured by these gorgeous Highland Cows.

I hope to paint a full portrait later. The cow as I captured her poised on the path. This particular lady is named Sandy

Notes

eye too high Need to move down.

I sit in the Quiet Corner of the Abbey on this Sunday and my heart is full.
I am at once both hushed and ebullient within my spirit.
Draw us into your love Christ Jesus. Deliver us from fear.

Today the Iona Community Worship Book reads:

If we were not so single minded about keeping our lives moving
and for once could do nothing,
perhaps a huge silence might interrupt this sadness
of never understanding ourselves
and threatening ourselves with death.
~ Pablo Neruda

I am the vine and you are the branches.
Whoever remains in Me and I in him will bear much fruit.
For you can do nothing without Me.
~ John 15:5

"in this chair
and by this window
Victoria, daughter of George VIIIth Duke of Argyll
dedicated her life to the glory of God in the service of the people on the island."

the sketch of the cloisters

in the Abbey is my favourite drawing ∪ I've done here. It is quiet and mystical and a bit eerie as well. It makes me feel exactly how I felt when I saw the cloisters for the first time.

This picture is, in fact, drawn from a photo. When my phone died in a rainstorm in January, I thought I would have to go without a camera during my time here, but John graciously lent me a small pocket camera to use and I'm very grateful for it. The weather has made drawing outside challenging to say the least. I have a hard time sketching with any type of glove on (even the fingerless type) so I can usually only draw for just a few minutes before my fingers are too frozen to move.

The angle of this illustration is also only possible because I used a camera. I was able to zoom into the carvings in a way that allowed me to render the details I wanted to capture. I feel like I am learning to give myself permission to use whatever tools work best for my drawing process. There is a freedom in this as well. It seems freedom is the emerging theme of this residency. How lovely.

inside the cloister...
shapes
faces

The starlings swirl & dance
under a clare & brilliant
winter sun.

twilight

on Iona is strangely different than other places
perhaps when it is overcast
light falls heavier
than when we are graced with a sunny sky

I think it is also due to the absence of loud sounds

this city girl is not used to it
my ears throb and flex waiting for... what?
I'm not sure...

the soft fall of rain is lovely
the best kind of sound

an
Afternoon
tea &
scone at the
Argyll hotel
... delicious

I'm from Portland, Oregon, where we take our coffee seriously. I had no idea how much power tea has in the UK, where a cup of tea ('a cuppa') seems to be the solution to every problem.

Feeling cold? How about a cuppa? Feeling tired? A cuppa will perk you right up! Bad breakup? A cuppa will make you feel better. Bored? Make a cuppa… at least that way you will have something to do. And if you're making one, make me one too!

When I was on Iona in February, not a single hotel or cafe was open. Now, in November, the Argyll Hotel on the waterfront offers lunch and tea from 10 to 2, Wednesday through Saturday. All of us at the hostel plan our days around 'going into town' and lunching at the Argyll. The real treat is ordering a scone and tea. Thick clotted cream and jam served with a buttery, flaky scone the size of a fist. It is a true test of character not to gobble the whole thing down while waiting for your tea to steep.

I think I have been converted to prefer a cuppa in the morning over that traditional American mug of coffee. A big cup of Earl Grey, creamy with milk and honey, is my favourite. I turn on the electric kettle if I'm feeling cold, or tired, or heartbroken or even bored…

nothing but a cuppa will do

During these past fourteen months traveling abroad,
I longed to reconnect with

the idea of home

Not 'home' as in the city or house you live in,
but 'home' as in the place where you feel safe and held and known.
The place that is made up of contentment and simple joys and where, bit by bit,
breathing comes easier and you realise that you can be exactly who you are,
and that you are whole and loved and beloved.

Hmmm… sounds like heaven.

I find 'home' on Iona;
in the warmth and friendship and encouragementof the people who live
and work and flow through the simple green building in this drawing.

I love so many things here:
the long, weathered wood table where we eat our meals,
the comfy, inviting couches under the big glass windows overlooking the sea,
and especially the community of people that surrounds me.

I hope you someday have the opportunity
to find yourself burrowed into one of these couches,
having a cup of tea and a conversation,
and encountering unexpected grace.

Encountering a bit of heaven.

Fingal's Cave
Isle of Staffa

During my stay on Iona in February I hadn't even thought about trying to visit **the isle of staffa** as there are no boat tours in the middle of winter. But the Monday I return to Iona in late October is different. It is a day full of vivid shades of blue woven through ocean and sky. The day is perfect and calm and it is the last week of tours before the boat is housed for the winter. I drop my bag off at the hostel and arrive at the pier just in time. A group of twelve of us head off to Staffa, in the back of an open tour boat, our eyes blinded by the bright autumn sunshine.

It's almost impossible for me to describe this wonderful and fanciful freak of nature. Many people have heard of Giant's Causeway in Ireland; Staffa is composed of the same kind of stone, columnar basalt. The name Staffa is said to have originated from the Old Norse for 'Pillar Island' because the rock formations reminded the Vikings of their houses, which were made from vertically placed tree logs. It's hard to believe the layers upon layers of pillars are real, and even harder to believe they are made of stone.

As I draw a small section of them I could be creating an architectural drawing of a cutting edge modern building. The island itself feels like an abstract stage set that has been suddenly discarded. The set designer went crazy constructing his masterpiece and then, at the eleventh hour, the producer decided he wanted something classic and the whole thing was tossed into the ocean. Paint was spilled and thousands of carefully assembled cubes and columns all tipped and broke and scattered.

We use the handrail attached to the side
of the cliffs and carefully wind our way
around the outside of the sheer rock walls
so that we can enter into the main cavern,
called *fingal's cave*

As I sit inside the opening, I am stunned and awestruck. The chamber itself is a marvelously eccentric futuristic cathedral that Gaudi would have felt at home in and secretly wished he designed.

These are the moments when traveling feeds the soul, when wonder and delight rush and tumble over and through you and all there is to do is bask in the magnificence of what you are seeing or experiencing. It can be an island, or a mountain, or a temple, a new friendship, or even a plate of food. If you are really lucky, it can be a cathedral emerging from the middle of the sea, gleaming under a late October sun.

Inside Fingal's Cave

grey
quiet
days

stack one upon another
still afternoons with shades of silver distilled to white where sky bleeds into sea

the horizon line is the palest thread out in the distance
other islands lost in heavy wet mist

I always marvel at the ivory sand on this, the north side of Iona
somehow it sparkles, despite the lack of light and sun

the water is calm as well
turquoise shallows moving to darker sapphire depths

I imagine this beach has always been this way
untouched and empty

only my silent feet to tread the sand

The rocks in the sand
on Iona are works of
abstract art. A slash
of salmon
amongst
an otherwise
neutral
palette

jane's
house

overlooking Eilean Annraidh
(Island of Storm)

I pass Jane's house every time I walk back to the hostel. Its stark white structure looks out over the water, defiant and solitary in the winter storms that sweep along the Hebrides. One afternoon, I make my way along the rocky beach below the house and realise I need to cut through Jane's property to escape being trapped by barbwire fences. Upon my exit, I strike up a conversation with one of the neighbours who is out walking her dog, and begin to learn the rich history of Jane's house.

Before coming to Iona, I spent a few days in Glasgow, where I visited the Hunterian Art Gallery. The Hunterian boasts a wonderful collection of works by the Glasgow Boys, Whistler and many others. A few of the paintings on display were created by Scottish Colourists Francis Cadell and Samuel Peploe. These paintings are views off the north end of Iona, views I also grow to love in the time I spend here. From about 1912 until at least 1933, Cadell visited Iona virtually every summer, during which he produced vibrant seascapes and landscapes. Peploe started joining him in 1920, and they enjoyed commercial success with the pictures they painted from the shores of the island.

What I discover in my conversation is that Cadell and Peploe had rented Jane's house every summer they lived on Iona. The next day I return to the grassy hill above the house and sit with my body facing north and sketch until my fingers freeze. I am mesmerized by the very same light and colours as those long ago artists, and there is something about this experience that pulls me out of time and into history.

Even though Jane's house has been renovated and added to in the century since Cadell started painting here, I can still imagine him out in the grass near the garden, paintbrush at the ready. I see his forehead furrowed in concentration, eager to capture the ethereal beauty spread beneath his feet. I am quiet. I don't want to disturb him. The light moves quickly, and it is time to work.

Ho! Everyone who thirsts,

come to the waters

And you who have no money, Come buy and eat.

Yes, come buy wine and milk without money and without price.

Why do you spend money for what is not bread,

And your wages for what does not satisfy?

Listen carefully to Me, and eat what is good,

And let your soul delight itself in abundance.

Incline your ear, and come to Me.

Hear, and your soul shall live;

And I will make an everlasting covenant with you–

~ Isaiah 55: 1-3

my view of the ruins & Mull ...
piece of the old Bishop's
house glowing in the
afternoon light

I like to walk across the island south to

columba's bay

when I think the blue sky wide enough to last through an entire blustery winter afternoon. Columba's Bay is where one has the best chance to find the famous Iona marble (also called 'Columba's tears'), beautiful chalky white stone traversed with pale serpentine green veins.

This bay, where Columba supposedly first ran his boat aground, is also the best place on the island for finding every other kind of colourful and patterned stone. The rocks from this area of Scotland are dated at over 2.7 billion years old and probably should be under glass in a museum. Instead, they sit in huge piles on the edge of the ocean—some wet and vibrant under the breaking tide, some dry and pale and sun-washed farther up the shore.

Every stone you find here would be unrivaled and the grandest of its kind on a normal beach. It would be pocketed and carried home to be placed on a shelf and revered for its unique colour, striping or shape. In Columba's Bay one can afford to be choosy, palming and admiring and then releasing. There is always something new gleaming just a few steps further down the beach.

A moody sky over
Columbas bay.
First day of sunshine
in weeks.

searching for lona
marble ...
loving the
texture & colour & light.

There is a labyrinth on the grassy area
that ends before the stones begin.
I quietly move through its winding shape
while the sun darts and weaves
through the clouds.

In the center
of the
labyrinth
stones of every shape and colour
have been stacked,
placed and cradled:
rocks,
shells,
a solitary feather.

I place my own treasure in the center.
It feels good and true to be a part of marking something;
to leave something behind.
I imagine that my pebble will still be here,
nestled amongst the others,
to be viewed and admired
when someone else comes to center,
on their own winding journey.

Iona Nunnery — (a small
late afternoon   piece) from rocks porch

In February I had my private retreat in the bothy, but now, in November, I am living in the hostel with a group of women, seven of us in total. We joke that we are from the nunnery, all but one of us single, cloistered together on this holy isle. I have met many amazing ladies during my travels, but on Iona, this just seems magnified. These beautiful, inspirational women share their art and their lives with me. We talk about fledgling projects and our hardest challenges, past and present. We peer into the future, sharing tentative hopes buoyed by encouraging words and kindness.

Marc, who works in the hostel, says that Iona allows his layers to shed. I want that too. I want to shed the things I've needlessly tied to myself over the past years. Sometimes I fear I need the title of 'artist' or 'illustrator' to give me worth.

My time on Iona has helped confront and then quiet these fears. They will always shadow me, but they don't have the power they used to. I am slowly learning to be confident in who I am as an artist, and step into a creative space that embraces *abundance not scarcity*

At the Abbey Graveyard
cloudy skies
graveyard stones leaning
into the winter

Erected in
loving memory
of
Mary McGinnis
died 24th July 1870

no
names
on the
crumbled
ones

"Faced with the madness of a world
that is capable of self destruction,
let us affirm

*the madness
of the cross*

of non-violence,
of the outstretched hand,
of faith that God still reigns."

~ Emilio Castro

I find this quote in the Iona Community Worship Book on
November 9, 2016

the hermit's cell

is one of those sacred spaces on Iona that is part of the pilgrimage route. People have continued to debate over the actual function and history of this ring of stones, some stating that it was only a cow shed, rather than a hermitage where Columba communed with the Divine. I like that it could have been used for either purpose, or perhaps both. On Iona the division between simple and sacred seems to fade.

This spot is one of my favourite destinations to find as I traverse the island. I always celebrate discovering it anew, because my innate sense of direction is usually rather weak. One sunny afternoon, I walk north from the Beach at the Back of the Bay in an attempt to feel my way towards the Hermit's cell. When I recognise the jutting rock that dominates the sky above the stones, I am quite pleased with myself. I promptly sit down inside the circle and begin to draw.

I think of my dear friend Joan when I see this painting because she loves it so much. When friends love your work, especially those that are artists themselves, it feels like a shot of pure inspiration to the soul. Thank you, Joan.

Port Ban
turquoise
water, spring
sunshine

The North End from the top of dun

I have always been fascinated by cairns, mounds of stones made by humans. The practise is thought to have originated as a pagan rite meant to invoke spirits who would protect travelers, but later it was Christianised and crosses were added. Cairns were often used as trail markers, as well as to indicate burial sites.

I drew this picture from the top of Dun I on the last day I spent on Iona in March. Dun I means 'hill fort' in Gaelic and is the highest point on the island. All of Iona is unfurled, from the brilliant aqua-marine waters surrounding Eilean Annraidh at the north end to the sweep of earth and rock that hides Columba's Bay at the southern tip.

While I was traveling in Wales in September, a month before I returned to Iona, I learned that my dear friend Cyndi's 19-year-old son Alex tragically died, leaving his mother in a deep, unfathomable ocean of grief. She decides to come to the UK to scatter some of his ashes. Alex had loved his first visit to Great Britain and she wants to fulfill his wish to return. I ask her to come north to Iona for a few days. She says yes.

Today, on the top of Dun I, I watch Cyndi weep as she writes a good-bye message to her son. I feel the morning sun warm my skin as she scatters Alex's ashes around the base of the pile of ancient rocks. This cairn will have the honour of being a burial site for a tall, beautiful, whip-smart boy who was incredibly loved and will be forever missed. Iona is famously said to be a 'thin space' between heaven and earth. In this moment, on this bright November morning, we feel Alex's spirit in the air, and the light, and the wind, and we know it to be true.

Today I awake and God is before me.

At night as I dreamt He summoned the day,

for God never sleeps but patterns the morning

with slivers of gold or glory in grey.

today I arise and christ is beside me

He walked through the dark to scatter new light.

Yes, Christ is alive and beckons His people

to hope and to heal, resist and invite.

Today I affirm the spirit within me

at worship and work, in struggle and rest.

The spirit inspires all life which is changing

from fearing to faith, from broken to blest.

Today I enjoy the Trinity round me,

above and beneath, before and behind;

the Maker, the Son, the Spirit together

they called me to life and call me their friend.

I find these words by Graham Maule

in the Iona Community Worship Book.

They seem written especially for this resting place.

My last
full day
on Iona.
Eucharisteo!

I paint this last scene on my final full day on Iona.

This beach, called the White Strand of the Monks, feels untouched. I am always startled to find the occasional tourist walking amongst the striated rocks and piles of seaweed. Usually I am alone and the shore is unspoiled, allowing my feet to be the first to sink into the sparkling white sand.

The waters directly off the beach are usually a rich turquoise, but on my last day, the sea glints completely silver in the afternoon sunshine. The winter sun makes its way towards the horizon, turning the distant hills a glowing rose-pink, their blush a striking contrast to the indigo of the Berg of Mull. As I sit on a large flat rock and sketch, I am very careful to write out what I am sensing and feeling and to make the necessary pen marks to capture the landscape.

The afternoon is mine. Drawing here is a kind of prayer. A meditation. A seeing.

Eucharisteo. The ache of my back as I perch on this rock. Waves gently settling onto white sand at the water's edge. Clouds, great sculptures, wild and puffy stacks of cotton softening as they move out over the Atlantic. Mild air and virtually no wind. A December day spilling over with grace.

My heart is full of gratitude. Iona, thank you for rest and respite before I return.

thank you for holding me

but 'ere
the world ends
iona shall be
as it was

special thanks

to my Iona family:
John, Joan, Jo, Luke, Emily, Marc,
Simon, Kate, Colette, Vapuu,
Vicki, Heli, Caroline, Jane, Rachel
and the folks at the Iona Craft Shop.
I loved sharing meals, sheep observations,
cups of tea, and dreams with all of you.

to Lissa Rasmussen, Elena Watanabe,
Bob Reid and Anneli Anderson
for your ace proofing, font, and photoshop expertise.
I'm so glad you're on my team!

to Christine and Kim Appleberry
for opening your home to me while I completed this book.
I am so grateful for your continued support of my creative life.

especially to John Pattison.
Your edits, insight, and attention to detail have made this book infinitely better.
Thank you for believing in me and my work.
It means the world.

kari gale

is an artist and writer
from Portland, Oregon
specialising in the documentation
of journey, food and travel.

She published her first book
'The Art of Walking: An Illustrated
Journey on the Camino de Santiago' in
June of 2015. You can find out more
about Kari, view her work, and
read her blog at karigale.com.

Made in the USA
Middletown, DE
16 September 2024

61040347R00049